my IDEA

a GUIDE to BRING YOUR VISION →to← LIGHT

WORDS by
ROD TUCKER

PICTURES by
RACHEL ELEANOR

SCHIFFER PUBLISHING

4880 Lower Valley Road · Atglen, PA 19310

Designed by Rachel Eleanor
Cover design by Rachel Eleanor
Production design by Danielle D. Farmer
Hand-drawn typography by Rachel Eleanor/Roboto

ISBN: 978-0-7643-6401-3
Printed in India

Published by Schiffer Publishing, Ltd.
4880 Lower Valley Road
Atglen, PA 19310
Phone: (610) 593-1777; Fax: (610) 593-2002
Email: info@schifferbooks.com
Web: www.schifferbooks.com

For our complete selection of fine books on this and related subjects, please visit our website at www.schifferbooks.com. You may also write for a free catalog.

Schiffer Publishing's titles are available at special discounts for bulk purchases for sales promotions or premiums. Special editions, including personalized covers, corporate imprints, and excerpts, can be created in large quantities for special needs. For more information, contact the publisher.

We are always looking for people to write books on new and related subjects. If you have an idea for a book, please contact us at proposals@schifferbooks.com.

Anything you can imagine you can create. OPRAH WINFREY

DEDICATION

This book is dedicated to everyone who has really great ideas.

CONTENTS

LIFE
CYCLE
of an
IDEA

WELCOME

Welcome to *My Idea: A Guide to Bring Your Vision to Light!*

Ideas begin as a twinkle in your eye, a spark, a moment of inspiration.

This book is an interactive journey with your idea.

This book will help you give your ideas legs and feed them until they are mature enough to be released into the wild.

In this book:

- You will build your ideas from scratch.

- You will shape your ideas by adding details and whittling them down to form.

- You will feed your ideas so that they can stand on their own.

- You will launch your ideas, and others will be inspired by what they see.

Let's get started,

Rod and Rachel

PART ONE
BUILD IT

No army can withstand an idea whose time has come.

— VICTOR HUGO

INTRO

Building your idea takes time.

Ideas start as sparks in our minds, and they need time
to grow and mature. Just like little seeds growing into
tall trees, ideas need to be watered, cared for, encouraged,
and loved.

Ideas need to be built.

Plant your idea in this section. Watch it grow and become
something bigger than the spark in your mind. You might
surprise yourself with how creative you are, and your idea
might surprise you with a life of its own.

Building an idea is where the journey begins.

Spend some time sitting with your idea. Talk to it.
Dream with it. See what kind of foundation can be laid.

What is?
my idea?

What is the PURPOSE of MY IDEA?

PURPOSE

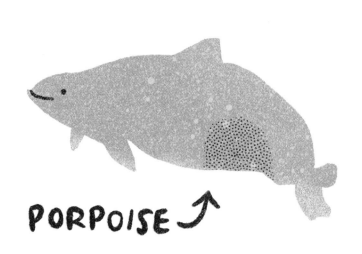

PORPOISE ↗

Write 5 sentences DESCRIBING my idea:

1.

2.

3.

4.

5.

Whom and HOW DOES MY IDEA HELP?

Where did my idea come from?

Why am I
excited
about my
idea?

3 PEOPLE
I AM EXCITED TO TELL ABOUT MY IDEA.

3 Words that describe my idea:

_____

What do I
want people
to say
about my
idea?

What makes
my idea
UNIQUE?

How will my
i dea help people?

What is
INSPIRING
about my
IDEA?

MY IDEA

MY
IDEA

↳ make connections

How will
people use
my idea?

How will my
idea make
people FEEL?

chills →

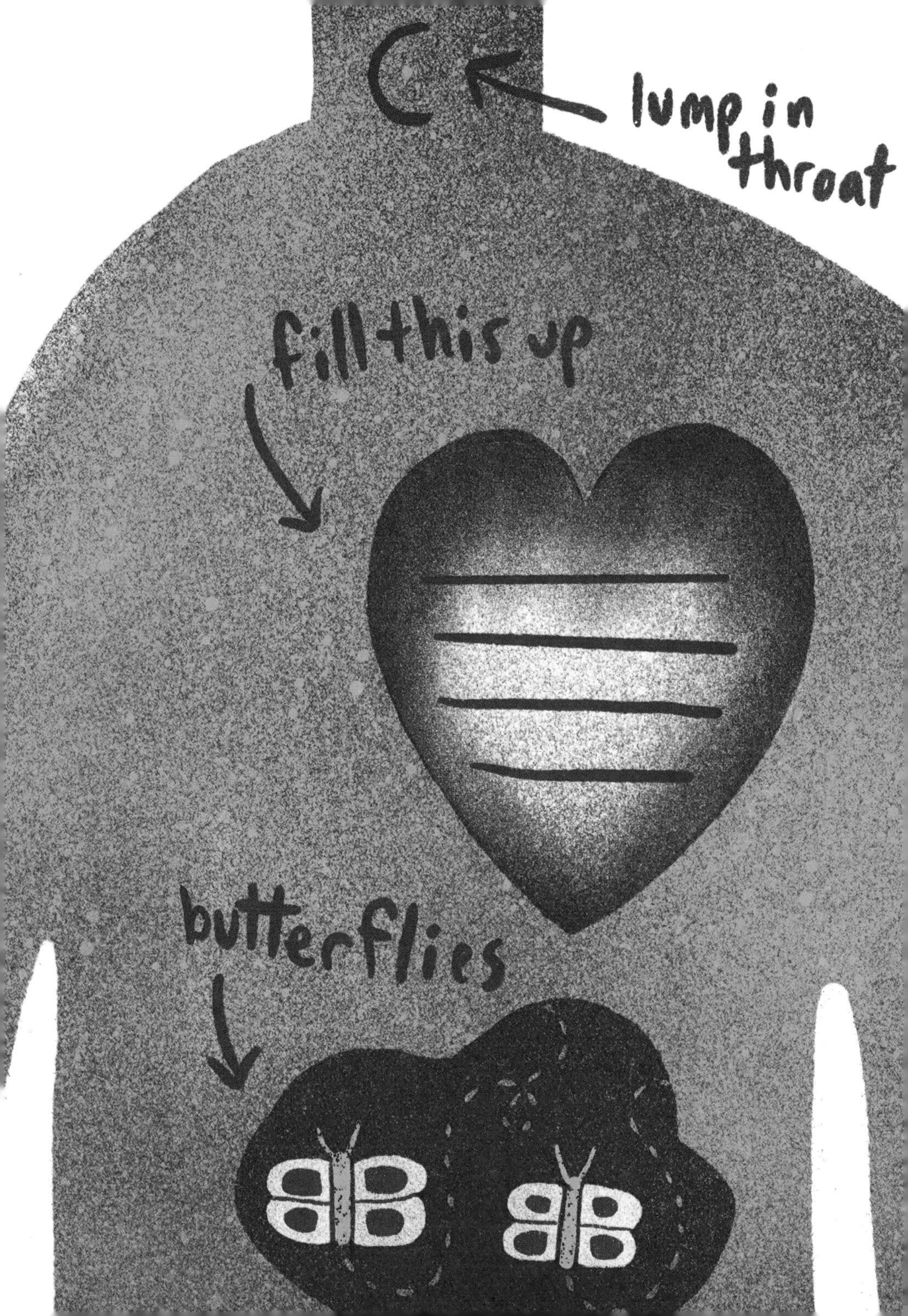
lump in throat
fill this up
butterflies

Who is <u>NOT</u> going to like my IDEA?

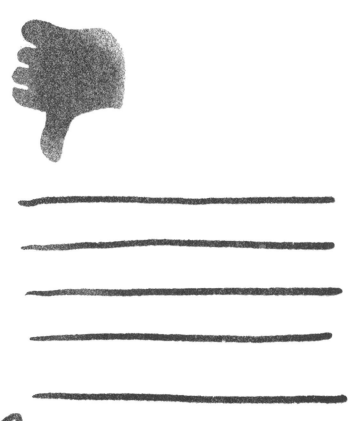

_____

_____

_____

_____

_____

ask them questions, too!

Who _is_ going to like my IDEA?

_____

_____

_____

_____

_____

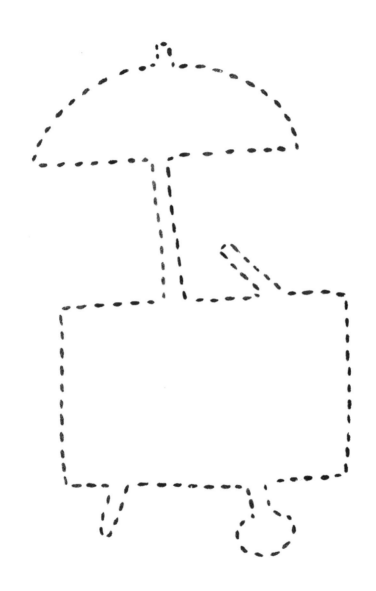

What does
the FINISHED
product look like?

What other ideas does this idea SPARK in me?

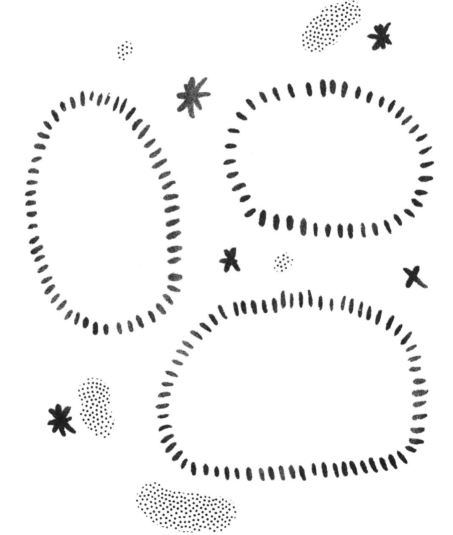

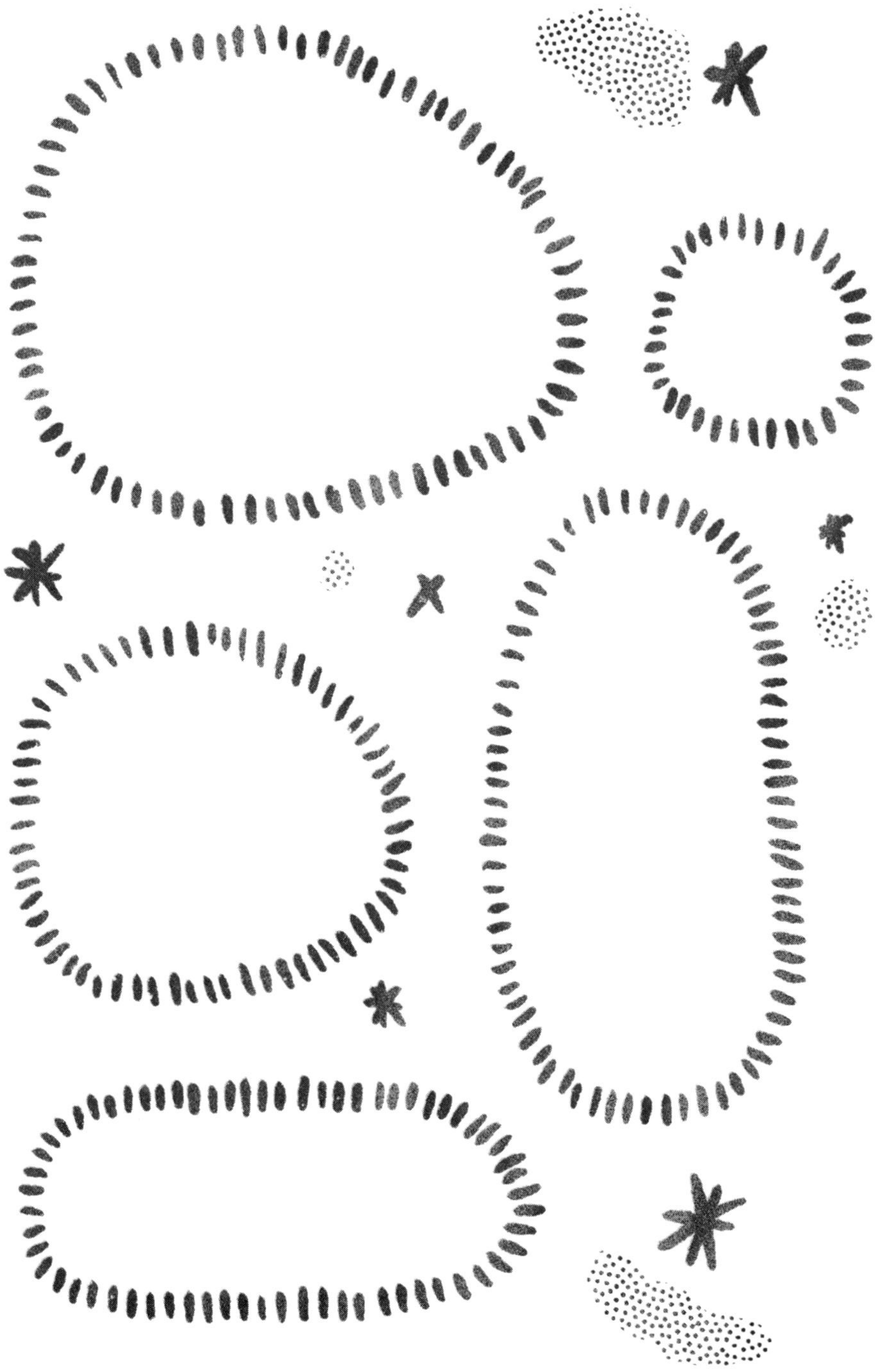

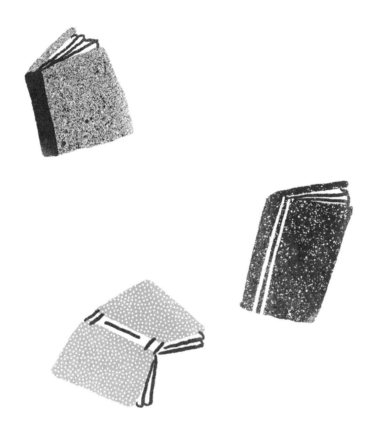

What RESEARCH do I need to do?

What am I willing
to risk or sacrifice
for this idea to take shape?

What ideas
are similar
to my idea?

What did they say?

Where
and when am
I going to work
on my idea?

What are my
fears around
this idea?

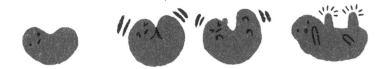

PART TWO
GIVE IT LEGS

For an idea that
does not at first
seem *INSANE,*
there is no hope.

— ALBERT EINSTEIN

INTRO

Building your idea takes time.
Shaping your idea takes courage.

Sculptors throughout history have stated that if you
want to chisel an elephant out of a stone, you do not
chisel out an elephant. Instead, you remove everything from
the stone that is not an elephant.

Then you have an elephant.

Shaping your idea means taking away everything that
does not help your idea take form.

This can be a difficult process, but the work is necessary.

Shaping your idea means giving it legs.

You want your idea to be able to move and breathe on its
own. You want your idea to show you what it wants to be, and
then you want to help it get there.

Shaping your idea means taking the necessary time
to work with what you have and turning it into what could
be.

This means giving your idea legs so that it can begin learning
to walk on its own.

Do research.

What did you find?

Write an
ELEVATOR
pitch.

What would
make my idea
better?

When do I want my idea to be finished?

How can my idea
succeed outside
my influence?

What needs
to happen to
make my idea
great?

Rewrite
my elevator pitch.

Picture a successful
launch of my idea.

where
am I?

Who is there?

How does it feel?

What I
LIKE

What I
WANT

What I DON'T LIKE

What I DON'T WANT

PART THREE
FEED IT

I had no idea that history was being made. I was just tired of giving up.

— Rosa Parks

INTRO

Shaping your idea takes courage.
Supporting your idea takes patience.

When you begin feeding your idea, it begins
to get stronger and gain momentum.

Time, energy, and intention spent with your idea
cause a better and more unique idea to emerge.

It is important to feed your idea with the right amount
of motivation and resources to make it grow into an idea
ready to launch.

People, money, and time are some of the food your idea
needs in order to grow into something that can be good
for the world.

Be patient.

Living things grow slowly.

Ideas also grow slowly.

But when an idea is fully grown, it can become
so much more than a twinkle in your eye.

Who might endorse my idea?

How will I
promote my
idea?

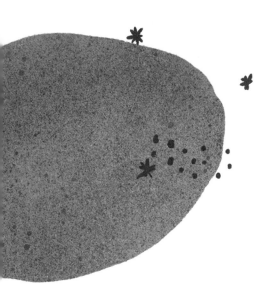

Where do I
promote
my idea?

Whom do I need to make this idea a reality?

Who is my audience?

Who is going to
support me financially?

Who is
going to
edit my idea?

Whom do I trust with my rough draft?

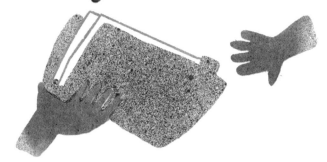

What do I need
to make this idea
a reality?

☑ GRAPPLING
      HOOKS
☐ RUBBER DUCK
☐
☐
☐
☐
☐

What are 3 STRENGTHS of my idea?

1. _____

2. _____

3. _____

What are 3 TWEAKS I need to make?

1. _____

2. _____

3. _____

What has stopped
me from following
through on my ideas
previously?

How can I plan
for success with
this idea?

PART FOUR

RELEASE IT INTO THE WILD

IN A GENTLE WAY,
YOU CAN SHAKE
THE WORLD.

—MAHATMA GANDHI

INTRO

Supporting your idea takes patience.
Launching your idea takes risk.

Once you have spent enough time with your idea
it becomes part of you.

You learn to love your idea because of how much
you have invested.

The more you love your idea, the harder it can be
to release it into the wild.

You have seen the twinkle in your eye.
You have taken the time to give it legs.
You have fed it and watched it grow.

And now you are faced with sending your idea out
on its own.

Your idea may face rejection.

You might feel afraid of the criticism your idea
might receive.

This is all a part of the natural life cycle of your idea.

As you prepare to launch your idea, be proud of how
far it has come, and celebrate something that can stand
on its own.

What is the first step in making this idea a reality?

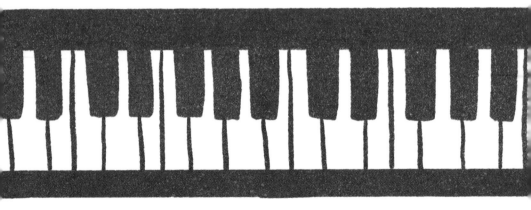

ORGANIZATIONAL TIMELINE

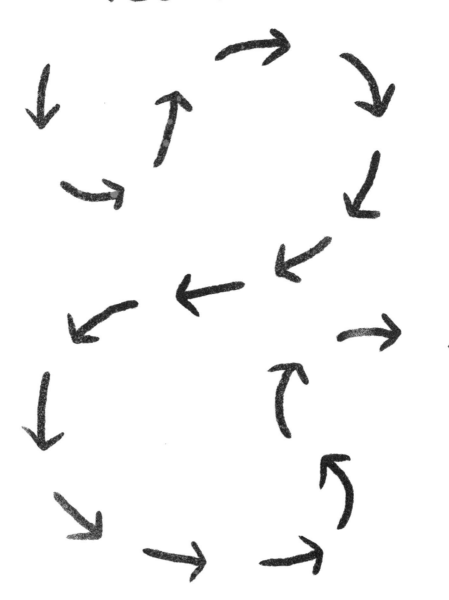

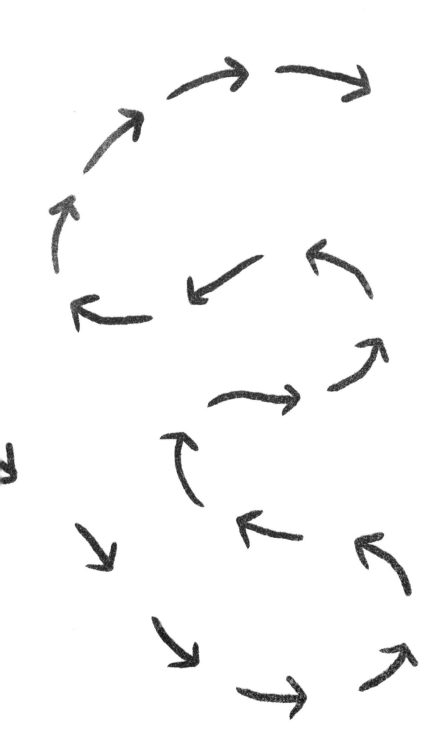

Where do I
need to focus
my energy first?

Whom will I check in with on my progress?

When I hit a snag
or feel like quitting,
what is my plan to
KEEP GOING?

How can I celebrate the completion of my idea?

When?

Where?

With?
whom?

AFTERWORD

Great work!

What started as a twinkle in your eye has become a living thing you are now able to release into the wild.

Continue to dream. Continue to challenge yourself. Continue to have ideas.

You are an idea-maker, a storyteller, and an inspiration to all those around you.

Continue to be you, and continue to build, shape, feed, and launch your ideas.

ACKNOWLEDGMENTS

To everyone who came together and helped
make *My Idea* a reality,

Thank you.

ABOUT THE
AUTHOR

Rod Tucker loves ideas.

He is a storyteller, inspirational speaker, author, and adventurer.

To learn more about Rod, visit rodtuckersays.com.

ABOUT THE
ILLUSTRATOR

Rachel Eleanor is a picture maker
and collector of stories.

To find more of her drawings,
visit rachel-eleanor.com.